Reading Maps

Written by Ann H. Matzke

rourkeeducationalmedia.com

Scan for Related Titles
and Teacher Resources

www.rourkeeducationalmedia.com

PHOTO CREDITS: Cover: ©Yarruta, ©Jolande Gerritsen; page 4: ©RTimages; page 5: ©btrenkel; page 6: ©filo; page 7: ©Oleg Troitsky; page 9: ©Jolande Gerritsen; page 12: ©PIKSEL; page 13: ©MarcelC; page 14: ©skodonnell; page 15: ©IndianSummer; page 17: ©Derek Punaro; page 18: ©DNY59; page 19: ©IHervas; page 21: ©michaeljung

Edited by:Jill Sherman

Cover and Interior design by: Tara Raymo

Library of Congress PCN Data

Reading Maps / Ann H. Matzke
(Little World Social Studies)
ISBN 978-1-62169-914-9 (hard cover)(alk. paper)
ISBN 978-1-62169-809-8 (soft cover)
ISBN 978-1-62717-019-2 (e-Book)
Library of Congress Control Number: 2013937308

Also Available as:

Rourke Educational Media
Printed in the United States of America,
North Mankato, Minnesota

Rourke
Educational Media

rourkeeducationalmedia.com
customerservice@rourkeeducationalmedia.com • PO Box 643328 Vero Beach, Florida 32964

Table of Contents

Reading Maps

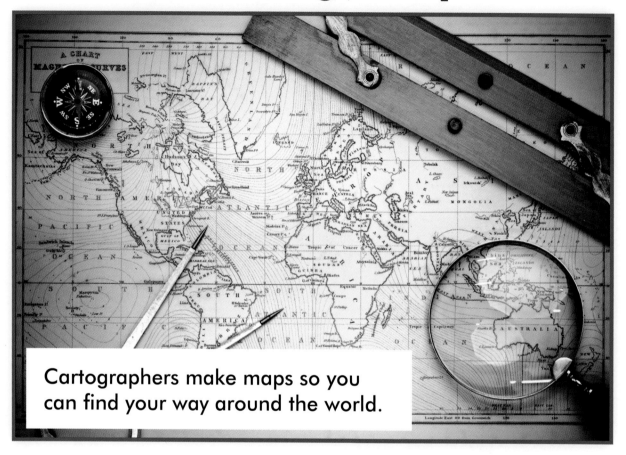

Cartographers make maps so you can find your way around the world.

A map is a drawing of a certain place.

Reading a map helps you discover places far away or nearby.

Like books, maps have titles. The title helps you pick the map you need.

Finding Your Way

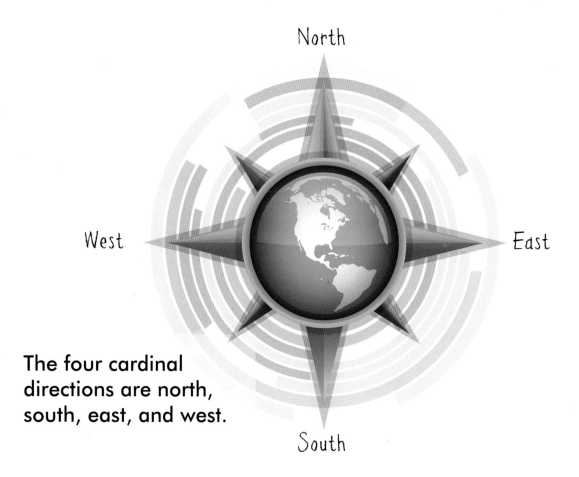

The four cardinal directions are north, south, east, and west.

A compass rose is a direction finder that always points north on a map.

North Pole

South Pole

North is toward the North Pole. South is toward the South Pole. East is to the right and west is to the left.

Highway		Gas Station
Waterway		Library
Train		Restaurant
Hospital		Parking
Fire Department		Hotel
Police Station		Camping

Maps use symbols. Symbols may be pictures, lines, colors, or dots.

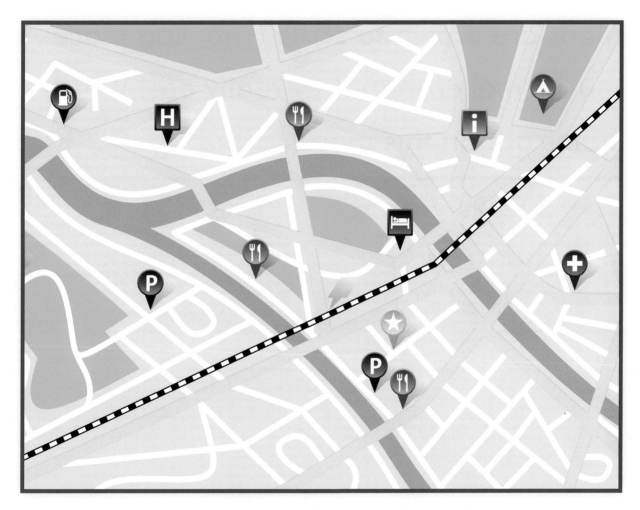

A map key or **legend** is a decoder,
explaining what the symbols mean.
Can you find the library symbol?

Maps are drawn to **scale**, showing places much smaller than they really are. Which states are on this map?

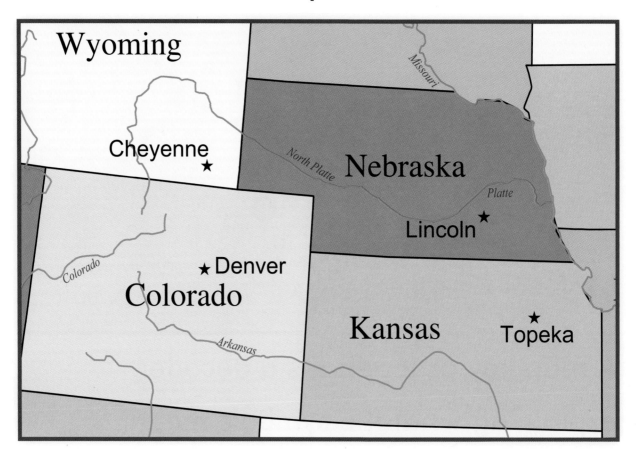

Wyoming

Missouri

Cheyenne ★

North Platte   Nebraska

Platte

Lincoln ★

Colorado

★ Denver

Colorado

Arkansas

Kansas   ★ Topeka

Political maps use lines to mark boundaries of states and countries.

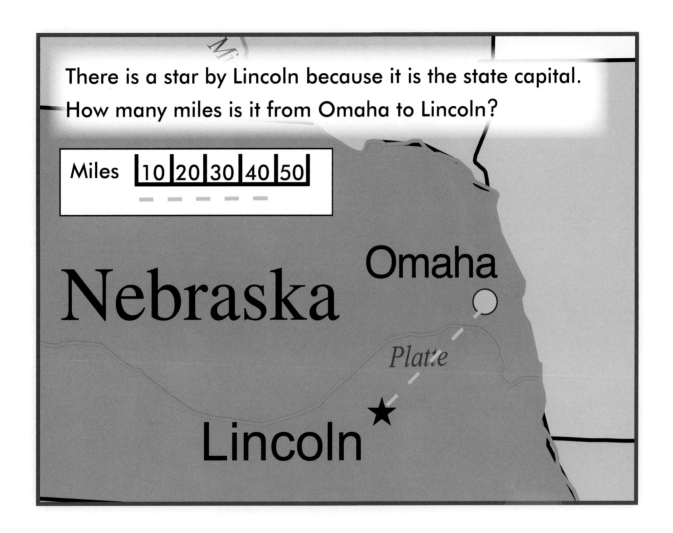

There is a star by Lincoln because it is the state capital. How many miles is it from Omaha to Lincoln?

Miles | 10 | 20 | 30 | 40 | 50 |

Nebraska

Omaha

Platte

Lincoln ★

A scale bar measures the distance between places on a map. It tells you the distance in the real world.

Globes

Globes show the truest shape of land and water. A globe is a small model of the Earth.

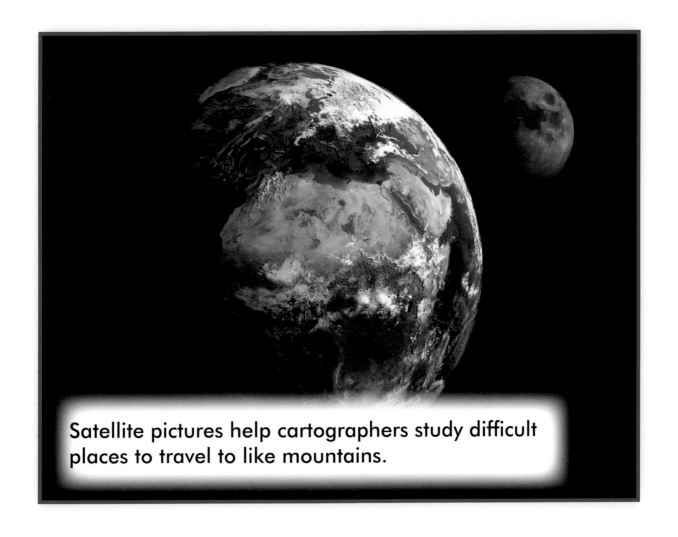

Satellite pictures help cartographers study difficult places to travel to like mountains.

The Earth seems flat, but pictures taken from space show the Earth is round like a sphere.

Look at the globe. The big green areas are land and the big blue areas are water.

Water covers more than half the Earth's surface.

The equator is an imaginary line around the middle of the Earth. It divides Earth into two equal parts called **hemispheres**.

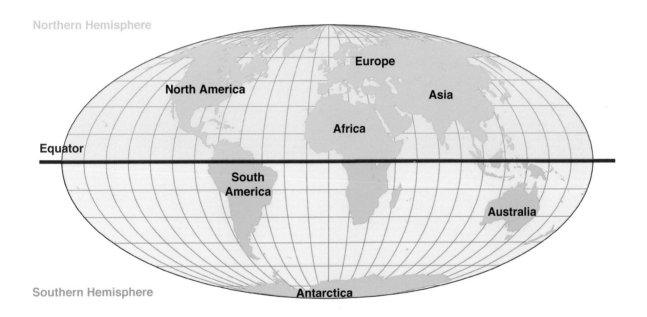

The equator is halfway between the North and South Poles.

Map **grids** make it easy to find a place.

The location of a place never changes.

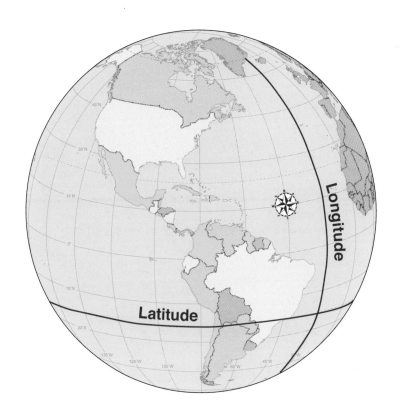

Lines of longitude run up and down.
Lines of latitude run around the Earth.

The treasure hunting game of geocaching uses map coordinates to find an absolute location and a prize.

Every place on Earth has a specific address called an absolute location.

Maps of All Kinds

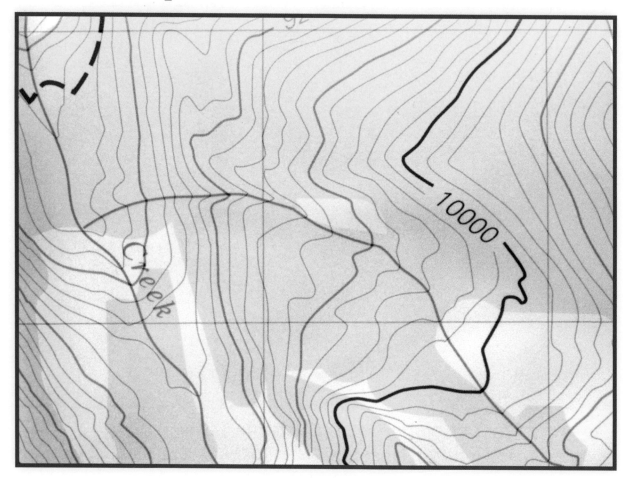

A topographical map uses lines to show high and low places.

Lines close together mean the land is steep like mountains. Lines further apart mean the land is flat like plains.

Climate maps show weather conditions.
Cartographers use color to show areas
that may be warmer or colder.

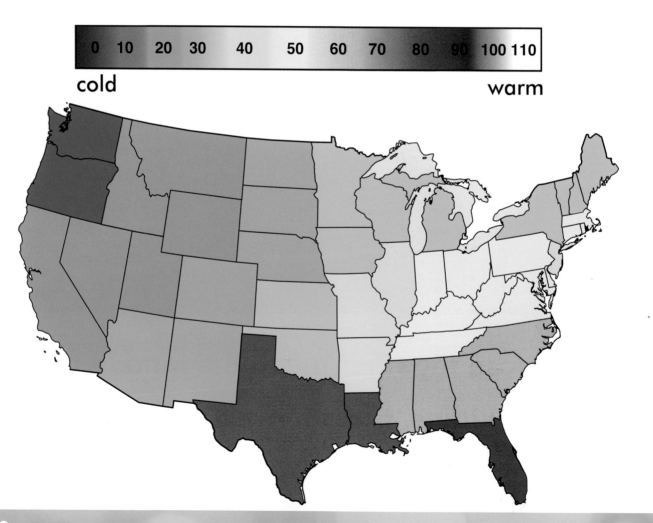

| 0 | 10 | 20 | 30 | 40 | 50 | 60 | 70 | 80 | 90 | 100 | 110 |

cold   warm

Pick up a map or spin a globe. Discover the world, far away or right nearby.

Try drawing your own map. Think about your house or school. Draw all of the rooms!

Picture Glossary

 **cartographers** (kar-TOG-ruh-fers): People who make maps.

 **climate** (KLYE-mit): The usual weather in a place.

 **grids** (GRIDS): A set of straight lines that cross each other to form a pattern of squares.

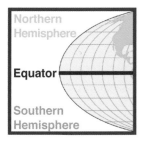

hemispheres (HEM-uhss-fihrs): The two halves of a sphere, like the Earth.

legend (LEJ-uhnd): The words written on a map to explain what different symbols stand for.

scale (SKALE): The ratio between the measurements on a map and the actual measurements.

Index

Websites

www.nationalgeographic.com/kids-world-atlas/maps.html

mapzone.ordnancesurvey.co.uk/mapzone/index.html

pbskids.org/arthur/games/elwoodcity

About the Author

Ann H. Matzke has an MFA in Writing for children and young adults from Hamline University. To locate Ann get out a map. Ann works as a children's librarian at the library in Cozad, Nebraska located on the 100th Meridian at 40.86 degrees North, 99.99 degrees West. Ann enjoys traveling and using maps to find fun places to visit.

Meet The Author!
www.meetREMauthors.com